Play-Along Series

As a young musician, I can remember how exciting it was to advance to each successive level because it meant I was getting to play with highly skilled musicians. That's the secret to improving your game—play with musicians who are better than you. Even though it can be a little intimidating at times, or even embarrassing a few times in my case, spending time paying your dues with accomplished players is a great way to accelerate your musical growth. Accordingly, I believe this book will provide you with a unique opportunity.

I count myself as one lucky guy, to lead a band with the caliber of musicians who make up the Big Phat Band. The players in the band are uniquely skilled and are without exception, masters at playing big band jazz in a variety of styles. They fearlessly attack the most difficult material I throw at them. Not only do they routinely achieve technical mastery of these charts but they also elevate the music to a new level beyond the notes on the page.

The Big Phat Band Play-Along Series gives you the opportunity to sit in with outstanding players to improve and measure your own ability to play in a big band. Make no mistake—the music in this book is challenging. The Phat Band has been playing these charts for years, and it *still* keeps us on our toes! But if you hang in there and keep at it, you will make huge strides toward the exhilaration and art of playing in a big band, along with becoming a stronger musician.

There are some minor alterations from the original published charts. For example, I added some inner trumpet lines to the trumpet and trombone books, and solo chord changes to all the books, so the horn players can solo. There are also a few notes that vary from the recorded tracks. Books are available for alto saxophone, tenor saxophone, trumpet, trombone, and drums.

The main goal of these books is to teach the art of ensemble playing. You will learn volumes of information about style, phrasing, tone, dynamics, technique, articulation, playing in time, Latin grooves, and a variety of swing styles as you play along and listen to the players in the Phat Band.

Participating in this series are the lead players from the Big Phat Band. These musicians are all world-class performers, and their guidance will be invaluable as you dig into this music.

- Wayne Bergeron is a one-of-a-kind lead trumpet player whose strong chops and great musicality make him one of the most in-demand musicians in Los Angeles.

- Bernie Dresel, one of the most musical and well-rounded drummers on the scene today, can play in any style, sight-read anything, and is also an accomplished orchestral percussionist.

- Eric Marienthal, a remarkable saxophonist, can be heard on recordings with the Chick Corea Electric Band and the Rippingtons, as well as on many recordings under his own name.

- Andy Martin, a superb improviser and one of the most facile trombonists in Los Angeles, sets a new standard for jazz trombone.

Since improvisation is an important facet in jazz, I have included chord changes for the solo sections in the saxophone, trumpet, and trombone books. The play-along recording has the solos mixed out so that you can jump in and blow! Selected transcriptions of some of the solos recorded by various band members are included in the saxophone, trumpet, and trombone books. You can use these transcribed solos to study, practice as etudes, or simply play in the solo sections. On the drum book audio recording, the original horn solos have been kept intact so you can play off the soloist. In addition, a Q&A session with Bernie Dresel and myself discusses aspects of big-band drumming.

To get the most out of the companion audio, you can of course use headphones as you play along with the tracks, but for me, the most realistic acoustical environment is to listen to the music through speakers with your ears unhindered by headphones. The key is to be able to hear yourself as well as everybody else in the band, and headphones can sometimes prevent you from hearing yourself well enough unless you take one ear off.

I have a policy in the Big Phat Band: on our gigs we come to play. The band works hard, no one makes excuses, and every player goes for it every night, all the while havin' a blast. I hope you have fun working with this book and it helps you grow as a musician.

www.gordongoodwin.com

Gordon Goodwin's Big Phat Band CDs—*Swingin' for the Fences, XXL*, and *The Phat Pack*—are available on Silverline Records (www.silverlinerecords.com)
Photography by Rex Bullington (www.Rexbullington.com)
Additional photos by Tessa Viles and Linda Griffin

Editor: Pete BarenBregge
Production Coordinator: Sharon Marlow
Art Design: Thais Yanes
Engraving: Rick Fansler

ONLINE ACCESS INCLUDED
AUDIO
WITH TnT2
Tone N Tempo Changing Play-Along Software

Stream or download the audio and software for this book. To access, visit: **alfred.com/redeem**

Enter this code:

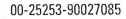

00-25253-90027085

Alfred

CONTENTS

	Page #	**Demo track**	**Play-Along track**

Full-version CD and DVD dual disc of all of these titles are
available from your favorite music store.

Visit: www.silverlinerecords.com

GORDON GOODWIN – As a three-time Emmy winner and a multi-Grammy nominee, Gordon Goodwin could say he has fulfilled his dreams and achieved all of his goals. But that isn't the case—not by a long shot. The composer/arranger released his second album, *XXL*, in September 2003, receiving three Grammy nominations for Best Large Jazz Ensemble Album, Best Instrumental Composition ("Hunting Wabbits"), and Best Instrumental Arrangement with Vocals ("Comes Love" with Brian McKnight and Take 6).

It all begin at the tender age of five, when Gordon Goodwin began composing from the music he heard in his head. Not just snippets or melody lines, but whole compositions from beginning to end. He wrote his first big band chart, "Hang Loose," at the age of 13. This almost preternatural talent made him stand out in the jazz world and brought Goodwin to the attention of music supervisors and producers.

Within the television and film industry, Goodwin's writing has garnered him three Emmy awards and six Grammy nominations. His cinematic scoring and orchestration can be heard on such films as *National Treasure, The Incredibles, Bad Boys II, The Majestic, Con Air, Gone in 60 Seconds, Enemy of the State, Remember the Titans, Star Trek Nemesis, Armageddon,* and the classic cult film *Attack of the Killer Tomatoes.*

Throughout his career, Goodwin has built a larger-than-life reputation for his composing, arranging, and musical instrumentation skills. Christina Aguilera, Quincy Jones, Mel Torme, David Foster, Toni Braxton, Ray Charles, Sarah Vaughan, Brian McKnight, and Johnny Mathis are just a few of the artists for whom he has written for, recorded and performed. In addition, he has conducted with world-renowned symphony orchestras in Atlanta, Dallas, Utah, Seattle, Toronto, and London.

Goodwin combines all of these talents as leader of L.A.'s most exciting big band jazz ensemble, **Gordon Goodwin's Big Phat Band.** Established in 2000, the band released its debut record, **Swingin' for the Fences** (Silverline Records), which made history as the first commercially available DVD audio title ever released and the first DVD audio title to receive two Grammy nominations.

Building on the tremendous success of their first album, Gordon and the boys returned to the studio and raised the ante, along with the roof. **XXL** is an exciting blend of jazz styles that stretches the boundaries of the big band genre. Along with his usual stable of L.A.'s finest musicians, including Eric Marienthal, Wayne Bergeron, Andy Martin, Bob Summers, Brian Scanlon, Luis Conte, and Bernie Dresel, this album features both legendary and contemporary guest artists. R&B great Brian McKnight teams up with vocal group Take 6 on the '30s classic "Comes Love," legendary crooner Johnny Mathis provides a knockout performance of "Let the

Good Times Roll," and Take 6 takes the lead on Goodwin's arrangement of "It's All Right With Me." Jazz greats Eddie Daniels, Michael Brecker, and Peter Erskine are also guest soloists on the record. The bold arrangements coupled with memory-evoking yet modern music are heart-stopping.

Sold-out L.A.-area performances by Gordon Goodwin's Big Phat Band are testimony to the genius of Goodwin's music and have earned the group high critical acclaim and praise: "The Big Phat Band has established itself as one of the Southland's most craftsman-like hard-swinging large jazz ensembles, galvanized by Goodwin's witty and insightful arrangements and compositions." —Don Heckman, *Los Angeles Times.*

The Big Phat Band's third CD, **The Phat Pack,** is scheduled for release in the spring of 2006, on Silverline Records.

Acknowledgments

Keeping a big band operating is a huge endeavor, and I am indebted to the many people who contribute to the band and to this series of books.

- The guys in the Big Phat Band—they are an amazing gift to any composer.

- To my friend and co-producer Dan Savant, who is a master at solving either business or creative issues, sometimes at the same time.

- To Pete BarenBregge, my editor at Alfred, whose vision and unwavering support really made this book happen.

- To my wife Lisa, who has made my passion her passion and knows firsthand the demands of running an organization like this one!

- To my multitalented assistant Linda, who hits every assignment out of the park—without exception.

- To Silverline Records, who believed in big band jazz when nobody else in the industry did.

- To our recording engineers and mixers Tommy Vicari, Mike Aarvold, and Gary Lux, who are responsible for the sparkling and punchy sound of our records. It's more than just pushing buttons; you have to get it, and they do.

ANDY MARTIN

Andy Martin, a gifted trombonist, grew up in a musical family. His father plays trumpet, and both of his brothers are professional musicians. He began playing with top artists at the age of 18. Presently he is widely regarded as a top jazz soloist, and is in high demand as a studio musician in Los Angeles. Andy is also a featured soloist on many outstanding recordings, including those of jazz greats Quincy Jones, Sammy Nestico, Bill Holman, the Poncho Sanchez Latin Jazz Band, Gordon Goodwin, Dave Grusin, Horace Silver, Vic Lewis's West Coast All-Stars, Clare Fischer, and many others.

Andy is the featured artist on a highly acclaimed CD recorded with the Metropole Orchestra in the Netherlands, conducted by Rob Pronk and John Clayton. There are currently five CDs available on which Andy is either leader or co-leader.

Throughout his young career, Andy has been featured in many big bands, including Louis Bellson, Jack Sheldon, Les Brown and His Band of Renown, Tom Kubis, the Phil Norman Tentet, and Frank Capp's Juggernaut.

Martin's studio credits are extensive. He has been recorded on dozens of motion picture soundtracks, including *Monsters Inc.*; *Planet of the Apes*; *Spider-Man*; *Big Fat Liar*; *Enemy of the State*; *Armageddon*; *Dracula 2000*; *Land Before Time (II, III, IV, V and VII)*; *Honey, We Shrunk Ourselves*; *Mother*; *Vegas Vacation*; *Mr. Magoo*; *Miami Rhapsody*; *Patch Adams*; and *Romeo Must Die*. His television credits include "The Academy Awards," "The Grammy Awards," "The Emmy Awards," "The Screen Actors Guild Awards," "The Golden Globe Awards," "The Tonight Show," and many others.

He has made recordings with Diane Schuur; Keely Smith; Tom Petty; Larry Carlton; Earth, Wind & Fire; Placido Domingo; Dianne Reeves; Arturo Sandoval; Paul Anka; Boz Scaggs; Barry Manilow; Lionel Richie; Neil Diamond; Brian Setzer; Steve Allen; Ana Gabriel; Vikki Carr; Simone, and the Hollywood Bowl Orchestra, to name just a few.

The title of his first CD, *Andy Martin Leading Off*, is a reference to his life-long love of baseball and the San Francisco Giants.

SWINGIN' FOR THE FENCES PERFORMANCE NOTES

By GORDON GOODWIN

This chart is based on the chord changes to "Sweet Georgia Brown" and is meant to be an acrobatic display of trombone technique on a complex bebop line. So I recommend practicing the part from measures 33 to 64 until it is second nature. You don't really have to play this line very loudly because in this case it's more important to play in time and with accuracy. Listen closely to other members of the band who are playing with you here, like the tenor players, two trombones, and the guitar player. You should aim for a unified sound and approach. When you have a passage like this one to learn, begin slowly and work it up gradually.

The chords to this song are really fun to improvise on, and there are tons of jazz recordings you can check out where great players have soloed on these changes. Of course, it helps to have knowledge of the bebop vocabulary and the notes in the chords. Keep in mind when improvising that melody is king and is often more effective than a sheet of notes. The first improvising step is to learn and memorize the melody and the sound of the chord progression. Know this tune inside and out to really tear it up. Listen how the chords move in a dominant pattern—live it, learn it, love it.

After the solos, you have a shout chorus to get through beginning at measure 130. These figures require that you stay on top of the time. Keep the ensemble playing nice and mobile during the eighth-note passages. When the Phat Band is really listening to one another and playing tight, I love to listen to them play the tail end of this chart. There's nothing like 17 musicians firing on all cylinders! Check out Andy Martin's transcribed solo on page 58.

By ANDY MARTIN

"Swingin' For the Fences" is a great swing chart, but I warn you: It is really fast. The opening chorus is trombones and tenors playing a unison line. Practice this line slowly with a metronome to make sure you're very precise with the time feel, especially on the opening chorus. Believe me when I tell you that trombonist Charlie Morillas and I spent some serious time practicing this line with the metronome. In measure 33 be careful not to come in early on the "and" of beat 4. Listen carefully to the hi-hat for the correct time feel. In measure 47, beats 4 and 4 "and," I recommend playing those Ds in a slightly flat 4th position. If measure 54 is a problem, ghost the "and" of beats 1 and 2.

In measure 63 try playing the A-flats in 1st position. It's a little bit of a flat note, but if you play the A-flats in 1st position, and the C-flat in 2nd position, you can make that lick fairly easily.

The soli in measure 130 is the whole band, so it's important to listen to how the lead trumpet is phrasing. Keep the short notes short so you don't drag the tempo.

In measures 190 and 191 you have lots of A-flats, and if you play them in 1st position, they're going to sound flat, so make sure to play them in the natural 3rd position. As a rule, any time you can, play them in the 3rd position.

SWINGIN' FOR THE FENCES

DEMO 1 | **PLAY-ALONG** 2

Trombone

GORDON GOODWIN (ASCAP)

LA ALMEJA PEQUEÑA
PERFORMANCE NOTES

By GORDON GOODWIN

When you play that melody at measure 19, you are recreating one of the classic sounds in jazz: the tenor sax and trombone in unison. Man, I never tire of that sound! But you must phrase and play in tune with the other guys in the band, so listen up!

Latin music requires precise rhythmic interpretation. The time must be locked and secure. Once in a while the ensemble may lay back on a figure for effect, but that kind of thing works only in contrast to the more strict interpretations that precede it. For example look at measures 97 and 238 where the triplets are an attempt to loosen things up a bit in the midst of all the straight eighth notes going on throughout the chart.

When soloing on this tune, you should remember the inherent passion behind all Latin music. In other words, go for it! Check out Wayne Bergeron's and Andy Martin's solos on the Phat Band's CD The Phat Pack. Both guys do a great job of playing exciting yet musically intriguing solos. You can check out Andy's transcribed solo on page 60.

After the solo section, you begin a long vamp in measure 153 that needs to start softly and build as each independent horn part is layered on. Everybody should be aware of how their individual part fits into the whole, not only here but also at measure 195, where the melody jumps from section to section. Maintaining the proper balance in a passage like this takes teamwork and an awareness of not only your specific part but also of what's going on around you.

I hope you have fun with this tune and that you avoid all clams, large and small!

By ANDY MARTIN

"La Almeja Pequeña," means the "The Little Clam," "clam" being slang for a mistake in the music, but you probably know that. When playing Latin music in general, I concentrate on putting the time right in the middle of the beat and tap my foot sometimes on top of my other foot in order to not make too much noise or distract anybody.

In measure 29, one option is to play to the F in a sharp 4th position to get the gliss up to A-flat. In a perfect world, there would be a consensus on how quickly to scoop the note in measures 31 and 53, and at this tempo you can't wait too long.

You will see meter changes in this chart, as in measure 69, which goes to 7/4, measure 70 to 6/4, and so on. Don't panic. I just try to keep track of the time by tapping my foot and counting from beat to beat. Of course, if you look ahead, make sure you're counting!

There are a few falls in this chart, for example measures 77 and 101, so make it a habit to always be sure you're matching the lead trumpet player on falls.

If you solo on this chart, go through and learn every single note up and down the chord. For instance, on an F7, play F, A, C, E-flat, and F, and then go back down. Then begin on the 3rd and play A, C, E-flat, F, A, and then back down. Then the 5th starting on C, E-flat, F, A, C, and so on. Work on that on every chord, making sure you know every extension.

LA ALMEJA PEQUEÑA
"THE LITTLE CLAM"

DEMO **3** | PLAY-ALONG **4**

Trombone

GORDON GOODWIN (ASCAP)

HUNTING WABBITS PERFORMANCE NOTES

By GORDON GOODWIN

The soli at measure 32 demands a wide range of expression—from short staccato figures in measures 32 and 44 to loud, powerful accents such as those in measure 43. Dynamics are a good thing, and it's a good habit to exaggerate them like the crescendo in measures 33, 35, and 37. Almost every measure has some kind of dynamic change, and if you catch these dynamics, the music really takes on interest and movement. Speaking of movement, you are relying on your own sense of good time, since the rhythm section is resting during this opening soli. Practice with a metronome and it will become second nature. Trust me, ya gotta do it. The first 86 measures of this chart should be played with no scoops or vibrato or other jazzy inflections. Save those for your improvised solo at measure 87!

By ANDY MARTIN

"Hunting Wabbits" is already a Gordon Goodwin classic. In this chart, the lead trombonist has to keep the time going along with all the section players. Listen for the bass trombone part two measures before measure 32, with those quarter notes leading into the trombone soli. It's important to get a nice, round classical tone on this chart. Make a nice crescendo in measure 33 and especially 35 to make that line work. Dynamics are always critical, but in this trombone soli, it is supercritical. Make sure you have your straight mute handy, because as soon as you're done with the trombone soli in measure 54, you have less than two measures to get into a straight mute for measure 56. I usually place my straight mute either to the right side of my stand, right next to me, or in my lap.

If any of these charts become a challenge to get up into the high register, a good way of building high register chops is to play arpeggios up as high as you can go and then try to get one note higher the next day until you can get that note. Keep on getting note after note after note, higher and higher and higher. Yes, it takes time and effort.

HUNTING WABBITS

Trombone

GORDON GOODWIN (ASCAP)

WHODUNNIT?
PERFORMANCE NOTES

By GORDON GOODWIN

If you've ever seen an old private-eye movie, then you understand the right feel for this chart—sneaky, bluesy, and too cool for the room. When the trombones state the recurring rhythmic pattern in measure 2, it should be quiet but with a hint of the power to come. That means play it soft but intense with a nice tight rhythm and put those quarter notes right on the beat. The mutes come out at measure 36, but it still shouldn't get too loud—save that for the build into measure 76. It should be strong at measure 76, but you're going to want to save some gas for those five huge chords in measures 88 and 89. The whole band's gotta pound those chords out—really cream 'em!

If you want to solo on this tune, keep it bluesy and cool with lots of sassy attitude. Try using a plunger mute.

After the solos, there's a sax soli that leads us into the shout chorus. As usual, here's where the brass section earns its money and gets all the glory. In measure 175, I like to hear those doits, big and nasty. Squeeze it as high as the tempo will allow. Now, the thing is, although measure 175 is the beginning of the shout chorus, we need to kick it up another notch at measure 191. And while we're at it, there are five more of those big chords waiting for us at measure 224. Hey, I'm not worried. You're up for it, right?

By ANDY MARTIN

"Whodunnit" showcases the ability of the trombones to really swing. From measures 60 to 88 there are a lot of Gs on the third ledger line above the staff, and it's important to play these notes in a sharp 2nd position to make sure they're in tune. And while I'm at it, F-sharps are best played in the sharp 3rd position to make that note in tune. Be aware that in measure 83 there's a shake on a high A-flat and then you come down to a subito p in 84—be ready. Always be on the watch for dynamics. For example, after the solo section, there's a big crescendo into measure 129 that is important and then you come right back down to mp in measure 130. In measure 157 consider playing that D on beat 3 in a slightly flat 4th position so you can make all of those first four notes in 4th position. More dynamics are always coming up, like the subito p at measure 167.

WHODUNNIT?

DEMO 7 | PLAY-ALONG 8

Trombone

GORDON GOODWIN (ASCAP)

24

COUNT BUBBA'S REVENGE PERFORMANCE NOTES

By GORDON GOODWIN

This chart starts out with one of the classic sounds in jazz: the tenors and trombones in unison. Play those rhythms nice and tight, and be sure to observe the dynamics in measures 2, 10, and 14.

The shuffle feel is one of my favorites—all you have to do is swing the eighth notes a little harder and it gives the music a nice forward movement. You will want to get the shuffle feel into your mind and body so that when the rhythm section drops during your soli at bar 92, the time doesn't lag. This soli is one of the more challenging that I've written, so heads up! Be sure to line up rhythmically with the bass trombone in measures 96–98 and get that tongue ready for the articulation in measure 101.

For the improv solo, I suggest getting used to hearing the roots of the chord progression and then learning the notes of each chord and any common tones. Then you can begin to weave through these changes and create some music of your own.

After the solos, you once again have the responsibility to keep the time going in measure 183. Be sure to watch the dynamics. The shout chorus at measure 244 is pretty slamming, and when you get to the last note, be ready to pop it with a nice big *sfz* accent.

By ANDY MARTIN

For "Count Bubba's Revenge," in measure 1 think about ghosting the very last note to make that high A to B-flat in measure 2 and the "and" of 3 in measure 10. Saxophonists have buttons that can move an octave, but we brass players don't have that option, so plan ahead.

I like to really dig into the swing feel at measures 5, 6, and 7, and 23, 24, and 25. Lead the way for the ensemble! Ghost the last note in measure 27, which is the same as measure 1. Be ready at measure 56 because this time it's harmonized and the lead trombone has the lead voice here. To me the most important part of the chart is measure 92, the trombone soli. Tap your foot if you must, but keep the time going with a really strong swing feel. This is also very important for the bass trombonist, because in measure 96 the bass 'bone has the counterline and counterbeats. Practice measure 99 slowly to make sure you hear the intervals, and get this line to live in the right spot in your ear and on the horn. In measure 101, I like to gliss those notes to make that line swing harder and move with the right time feel. For the entire trombone soli at measures 92 to 108, work it out with a metronome to make sure you're getting the right time feel, and practice it slowly, working up to the actual tempo.

Another important section is measure 183 after the solos, because the bass trombonist is playing on beats 1 and 3 and the rest of the section is on beats 2 and 4, so only the bones are playing time. Make sure you are on the boat regarding the time and feel; don't drag, don't rush—be precise with nice, short notes.

I worked hard on measures 253–254 because to go from the B-flat up to a high C and then make those intervals—C to G, B to F-sharp, B-flat to F to A—is difficult. To hear those pitches, play it slowly and work through it so you own those intervals. In measure 256, the quarter notes are long and accented. Check out the last note of the chart in measure 266, a long gliss with the slide but not a lip fall, just a straight gliss with a gnarly sound.

COUNT BUBBA'S REVENGE

DEMO 9 | **PLAY-ALONG** 10

Trombone

GORDON GOODWIN (ASCAP)

GET IN LINE
PERFORMANCE NOTES

By GORDON GOODWIN

Trombones have a unique challenge when it comes to playing funk music. The instrument doesn't lend itself naturally to fast, slick licks, so you will have to work on keeping up with the saxes and trumpets on this one. One of the great challenges of the trombone is to play with power and energy without sacrificing accuracy and fluidity. But Andy Martin and all the 'bones figured it out, and so can you. Listen and copy!

When playing a chart like this, you must commit to the stylistic parameters. Which means playing these licks with soul, tightness, and precision. Listen to Andy on the Phat Band's CD recording of "Get in Line" and you can hear how he and all the horn players support each phrase with a strong air stream. Many of the licks in this chart emulate a solo instrument or vocal, so as a group you must all phrase together as one perhaps even more so than on a traditional swing chart. Listen closely to the rest of the section to make sure all the articulations are the same, including the note lengths, the scoops, falls, pace of crescendos, type of vibrato, etc.

In "Get in Line," the lead trombone plays in a small ensemble composed of three saxes and two trumpets. In those settings, make sure to maintain a good blend, and not only with regard to volume, but it is here where your articulation should most accurately match the saxes and trumpets.

If you are soloing on this tune, you will find that the usual bluesy pentatonic licks work really well, but don't be afraid to try some new stuff. Listen to the sound of the root chord progression and become familiar with the notes in the chords. Whatever you play, it should have energy and feel good and funky. Have fun!

By ANDY MARTIN

"Get in Line," is a funky chart with a straight up-and-down feel—no swing. It's important in measure 20 when we have that scoop on the "and" of beat 3 to not let the time get behind. Stay on top of the beat as well as every other time in the chart that this lick occurs. There's a sax-like figure at measures 33 and 34 that's really cool if you can line it up with the saxophones. In measure 88 there is a background lick that goes from F to F-sharp to G. I start that lick in sharp 4th position on the F, the F-sharp in sharp 3rd position, and the G in sharp 2nd. All that makes the lick easier if you go straight up the slide. In measure 92 the trombones have a brief smooth section, so play the half notes as smoothly as you can and let them ring out right in tune—make the trombone sound shine. Measures 104 and 105 may need some work in the practice room. Play that line very slowly to make sure you hear those intervals. I really dig this chart because of the straight up-and-down feel but check out measure 143, with a different rhythm than you've seen before in this chart.

When I'm playing in the trombone section with the likes of Alex Iles, Charlie Morillas, and Craig Ware, it's very easy because I know everybody's going to be sight-reading everything perfectly and phrasing everything with me, so it's a great team effort. Teamwork is essential for a trombone section to sound good. A large part of teamwork is matching the lead player's volume, phrasing, intonation, time, feel, interpretation, volume level, and just about every note he or she is playing.

One of the keys to playing in a big band is listening for the time. Always listen for the bass, the hi-hat, and the overall time feel in the whole drumset, and don't be shy about tapping your foot, but don't let it bother your neighbor. When I play a jazz solo, I always try to play something rhythmically to start off my solo so the drummer will get interested in what I'm doing. Then the drummer will play off me, and the rhythm section will react to what the soloist is doing, and in turn the soloist can react to what the rhythm section is playing. The goal is to listen to each other.

GET IN LINE

DEMO **11** | PLAY-ALONG **12**

Trombone

GORDON GOODWIN (ASCAP)

GET IN LINE

HORN OF PUENTE
PERFORMANCE NOTES

By GORDON GOODWIN

The trombones have a supporting role in the first half of this chart, but when the tempo picks up at measure 84, it's time to get to work. For this book I have added some lines from the 2nd trumpet part to give you a chance to work on blending and playing some tough lines. You have a soli with the trumpet and tenor sax at measure 92, and you will need to start subdividing the beat in your mind as you play. This becomes really important at measure 100, where the band has an interesting syncopated figure that is actually easier to play than it looks. You will notice that there are plenty of places in this chart where you need to come in on the last sixteenth note of the beat—so don't be late! Examples of this can be found in measures 105, 107, 113, and 121, and just about all over this chart!

The solo section on this tune is hot, hot, hot. You're going to have to go for it, but remember to pace yourself. Your solo should have a good arc to it. There is a tradition of trombone players playing hot, exciting solos over this kind of groove, and you can check out what Wayne Bergeron did on the trumpet on this tune on our CD *XXL*. Solo-wise, energy is the key ingredient in this type of chart. Build, phrase, listen to the rhythm section and the groove, use snippets from the melody, and play off any backgrounds you might hear. Always feel free to incorporate motives from the melody in a solo. That is a simple but effective tool in creating a solo. Keep in mind that for a solo in a tune like this, the rule of showbiz dictates that you'll need to find your own special way to bring the crowd to its feet.

After the solos, things heat up even further, and we really bring it home at the key change in measure 165. Save some chops for this part so that the energy stays high and propels you to the end of the chart. Salsa music is the best!

By ANDY MARTIN

"Horn of Puente" is a feature for lead trumpeter Wayne Bergeron. Being a lead player in the brass section absolutely requires you to pace yourself to maintain endurance. Sometimes I'll pass my lead part to my section mate, at which time my role changes because as a second or third trombone player, I'm matching somebody else's lead interpretation.

This is a Latin chart, and that means a straight up-and-down time feel—not swing. Try to play right in the center of the beat and time.

Measures 66–74 is a long phrase usually played in one breath. So you must either tank up a really big breath before this phrase or possibly sneak a breath before beat 4 in measure 69. The crescendo from measure 73 to measure 74 is very important in this chart.

At measure 92 you're matching the trumpet soloist, so make sure you're going to support and match that part to the best of your ability. Time is especially important on the sixteenth notes, so don't drag, and make sure you're locked in with the rhythm section. This chart requires you to think about getting the right amount of air. For example, starting on beat 4 of measure 98, take a big breath so you can make it through the end of this phrase to measure 101. Measure 102 is only trombones, so play it strong and gnarly. Another phrase to gear up for is measures 124–127.

Practice the key change at measure 165, because you're playing the same licks but in a new key. You want to have the skills to play it in time and in tune.

HORN OF PUENTE

DEMO **13** | PLAY-ALONG **14**

Trombone

GORDON GOODWIN (ASCAP)

GORDON GOODWIN'S BIG Phat BAND

THE JAZZ POLICE
PERFORMANCE NOTES

By GORDON GOODWIN

Andy mentions that the rhythm section gets loud on this chart, and he is correct. But you know, rock 'n' roll is usually loud, and "The Jazz Police" is a rock chart that is all about the energy and the groove. It can be frustrating for a horn player in a typical rock band trying to compete with electric guitars and drums. So what are you going to do about it? The way I see it, you have three choices:

1. Never play that kind of music.
2. Use earplugs like Andy and many, many other musicians.
3. Build superstrong chops so you can keep it up and play this kind of music the way it demands.

Actually, Andy has chosen options 2 and 3. I think that's probably the way to go.

Just because this chart is slammin' throughout doesn't mean we throw all subtlety out the window. There are plenty of opportunities for (1) dynamics, like in measures 20, 36, 40, and 58, to name a few; (2) phrasing, for example, the accents and scoops in measures 9, 10 and 36 and (3) articulation throughout. These musical issues are all important in keeping your performance a nuanced one. Listen carefully during the unison sections: articulate, phrase, blend, and tune together with the rest of the band. In this style groove, it's vital to play all the eighth notes on top of the beat, never laid-back but always pushing forward. And toward the end of the chart, around measure 113, is where the whole band will have to dig down and pitch in to push this chart to the finish line. For the solo section, think rock, contemporary, and hot! The blues scale will work on these changes.

By ANDY MARTIN

"The Jazz Police" is clearly a high-energy rock chart. When you're playing a chart like this, usually the rhythm section is playing very loudly so it's important to be able to also play loudly but with control and not spread your chops. The tendency when playing loudly is to drag.

Ghost the "and" of beat 3 in measure 61. Follow the dynamics; play a nice, long fall in measure 89; and for the sixteenth notes in measure 96, try playing that F in sharp 4th position so you can play that lick in the correct time feel. You have a gliss from measure 112 to 113, so play the F-sharp in sharp 3rd position because the rest of the band is glissing without a slide. You won't need to go out to 5th to do that gliss, plus it will be more in tune in 3rd. In measure 121, I try to play those D-naturals in slightly flat 4th position to make that line a little smoother. But experiment with your own slide to make sure you can play it smoothly or try 1st position.

THE JAZZ POLICE

DEMO **15** | PLAY-ALONG **16**

Trombone

GORDON GOODWIN (ASCAP)

HIGH MAINTENANCE
PERFORMANCE NOTES

By GORDON GOODWIN

The trombones have an important job in this chart, and our lead trombone player Andy Martin nailed it when he spoke of staying on top of the beat. The eighth notes in measures 1–8 must be played in the proper place in time, or else it can really bog everything down. It becomes even more crucial in measure 125 because the rhythm section drops out, so listen carefully to the baritone sax player to keep the time poppin'!

The 1st trombone sometimes acts almost like a 5th trumpet. Check out measure 191. You must have good command of that register of the horn so you can play those figures cleanly and accurately. You can see that from measure 191 to the end, you are spending a lot of time above the staff, so it's going to require that your chops be in good shape so you will have the endurance and be able to lead your section to the end of the chart. Do your homework. You know the drill—all the long tones in the practice room really pay off when you are on the bandstand.

If you want to improvise on this tune, definitely check out Andy's transcribed solo on page 62. It's a textbook example of how to play an exciting, melodic solo that floats over the passing chords without resorting to mere blues licks. By the way, blues licks (the blues scale) will also work over these changes, but I hope you will go to the next level and search for your own lines, melodies, and other material to play on this song. As I mentioned earlier, the first step toward improvisation is to learn the melody and the sound of the chord progression.

By ANDY MARTIN

"High Maintenance," is a swing shuffle, and with a groove like this one, listen carefully to the rhythm section to lock in to the swing eighth notes and the strong backbeat on beats 2 and 4. Notice in the first few measures you have those hits on the "and" of beats 2 and 4—keep them tight and pop each note.

There are a few intervals at measures 23 and 24 with tri-tones, so make sure you hear the A to the E-flat and the C to the F-sharp and play measure 24 very smoothly with the written crescendo. In measure 28 catch the quick gliss into the "and" of beat 4 and don't drag. On the laid-back figures at measures 33, 37, and 41, make sure you're listening carefully to the lead alto and the lead trumpet to make sure you are phrasing exactly with them. Measures 45 and 46 offer some more tri-tone intervals—get those in your ear.

In measure 48 the trumpets fall longer than the 'bones because we need to hit the "and" of beat 2, so make sure you get off that fall fast regardless of what the trumpets are playing. At measure 133, there is a section where you might need to tap your foot to keep accurate time, because it's easy to drag or rush these notes. Play those quarter notes as straight as you can—no style needed. Play a short fall on beat 4 of measure 142 to make way for the sax soli.

HIGH MAINTENANCE

DEMO 17 | PLAY-ALONG 18

Trombone

GORDON GOODWIN (ASCAP)

48

High Maintenance

HIGH MAINTENANCE

HIGH MAINTENANCE

CUT 'N RUN
PERFORMANCE NOTES

By GORDON GOODWIN

Well, you might think you are off the hook in this chart as you sit there listening to the trumpets and saxes spit out all of those fast licks at the top of this chart, but just you wait! We've got some action for you after the solo section. Even though you have fewer active parts at the beginning, the phrases should be played nice and crisp, like at measures 5–8.

If you choose to solo on this track, you will find the chord changes actually allow a fair amount of freedom. For instance, the first 12 measures are essentially over a C pedal. You can play a blues scale if you want, but you can also float over that C pedal and play pretty much anything you want. Just go for it and keep that energy going!

Things get busy for you during the ensemble section at measure 119. Keep those eighth notes tight, although you can ghost certain notes, as Andy points out in his comments. Remember, though, that ghosting notes should be a device you use to enhance a style, not cover up a lick you can't quite play. Also, pay attention to the dynamics and accents in measures 127, 128, and 131.

The most challenging section to keep together is probably measures 151–160. All of those constant eighth notes can get a little mushy. But if you and the rest of the band have the licks dialed in and play them with precision, it's a pretty exciting section. Good luck!

By ANDY MARTIN

"Cut 'n Run." is a break-neck swing tempo chart. Make sure you listen to the hi-hat on this one and play crisp, short notes right on the beat. At measure 63 ghost the "and" of beat 1 and at measures 121 and 122. While you're at it, ghost the "and" of beat 1 in measure 122 along with the "and" of beat 2 in measure 125. Ghosting will definitely make these licks work better. When you play a tune this fast, don't play too loudly because that tends to bog down the time.

As you can hear, ghosting is important at this tempo. For the hot licks in measure 151, I usually play the B-flats on the "and" of beat 3 in sharp 5th position and the same thing in measure 152 on the "and" of 1. In measure 152, play that D-natural on the "and" of beat 3 in slightly flat 4th position. The same type of thing applies to the licks in 155, 156, and 169 on the "and" of 3. Likewise, in measure 181, ghost the "and" of 1, and in measure 195, ghost the "and" of beat 1.

Some final thoughts for playing with the Big Phat Band: Since I sit in the middle of the band, I always hear the lead trumpet right behind me. I follow every phrasing idea that he has because if I'm playing with him, I can't go wrong. In addition to the lead trumpet, other important aspects I listen for are the hi-hat and pitch from the piano and the bass. I put it all together and then I make my own interpretations within the style, tempo, and so on. As far as the job of playing lead trombone, I always try to play with a full breath of air, and I always try to sit straight up in my chair so I can make sure I'm supporting the air, because playing these charts requires a lot of energy.

Always be aware of the overall band intonation. I focus on the piano and bass to make sure that if the pitch is either climbing or going lower, I stay in the center of the pitch. The trombones are in the center of the band and can subtly tune the band. We 'bones usually have better intonation and must have good ears with only a slide in our hands.

CUT 'N RUN

DEMO 19 | PLAY-ALONG 20

Trombone

GORDON GOODWIN (ASCAP)

CUT 'N RUN

Gordon Goodwin's

INTRODUCTION TO SOLO TRANSCRIPTIONS

All of the discussion about the principles of ensemble playing is important, to be sure. But if you master all the techniques mentioned in this series, and even if you can play every one of these charts note-perfect and flawlessly, you aren't quite done. Because jazz requires an element of spontaneity, and it is that final element, the sense of freedom and exploration that we see in the great jazz innovators, that will make you and your ensemble come alive. This is rather intangible and is acquired only by listening and studying great improvisers—and there are plenty of examples both past and present. There are also many masterful technicians on various instruments, players who can dazzle you with their sound and mechanics. But what is rare is a musician who can do both. That is what I would ask you to aspire to. When playing in the section, you are a team member and submit to the will of the group, but when it is your turn to solo, you step up.

It is exactly this kind of musician we look for in the Big Phat Band. In this section of the book you will find transcriptions of solos played by various Phat Band members. You can listen to them (if you have our CDs), study them, and/or perform them yourself along with the track.

The selected trasnscribed solos are from these talented jazz musicians:

- Wayne Bergeron (trumpet)
- Gordon Goodwin (tenor sax)
- Eric Marienthal (alto sax and soprano sax)
- Andy Martin (trombone)
- Brian Scanlon (tenor sax)
- Bob Summers (trumpet)

SWINGIN' FOR THE FENCES
Andy Martin's Trombone Solo

GORDON GOODWIN (ASCAP)
Transcribed by BENNY GOLBIN

LA ALMEJA PEQUEÑA
"THE LITTLE CLAM"
Andy Martin's Trombone Solo

GORDON GOODWIN (ASCAP)
Transcribed by BENNY GOLBIN

HIGH MAINTENANCE
Andy Martin's Trombone Solo

GORDON GOODWIN (ASCAP)
Transcribed by BENNY GOLBIN